Hustling and Bustling
TRACTORS

WHEELS AND AUTOMOBILES

FOX EYE
PUBLISHING

A tractor is a machine that helps the farmer work the land.

Whatever the job, the trusty
tractor is there to lend a hand.

planting

ploughing

Tractors pull the farm machines
that harvest, plant and plough.

harvesting

Can you count the tractors in this picture?
How many have you found?

All tractors have a powerful engine.
The engine is super strong.

engine

It powers the tractor and farm machines
that the tractor pulls along.

A tractor has two huge back wheels.
These are chunky and wide.

wheel

They stop the tractor sinking in mud and help it not to slide.

cab

The farmer climbs a ladder. It is on the tractor's side.

The ladder goes up to the cab.
That's where the farmer drives.

The farmer uses controls inside the
tractor cab to make the tractor work.

The farmer plays music while he drives the tractor in the fields.

The trusty tractor carries some hay for the cows to eat.

The cows chase the tractor across the field.
They are hungry and run at full speed.

Here comes a tractor pulling a plough.
The plough digs up the ground.

tiller

Next the tiller breaks up the soil
before the seeds go down.

planter

This tractor is pulling a planter.
It sows the seeds in rows.

In summertime, the sun and rain
will help the crop to grow.

In Autumn, the harvester gathers
in the crop. It is fully grown.

harvester

As the sun sets, the trusty tractor carries the farmer home.

Bustling Words

The **cab** is where the farmer sits to drive the tractor. The tractor controls are inside the cab.

A **crop** is a plant that is grown for food.

An **engine** is part of a machine that makes energy.

A **harvest** describes crops that have been cut.

Hay is an animal's food. It is made from dried grass.

Machinery means machines. A machine is something that does a job. Cars, kettles and vacuum cleaners are all machines.

A **planter** is a type of farm machine that puts seeds into the soil.

To **plough** means to turn over clumps of soil. This makes the soil ready for planting.

A **plough** is a farm machine that is pulled by a tractor. It turns over the soil.

Powers means gives energy to something.

Seeds are tiny parts of plants that grow into new plants.

To **sow** means to put seeds into the ground.

A **tiller** is a farm machine that breaks up clumps of soil.

First published in 2024 by Fox Eye Publishing
Unit 31, Vulcan House Business Centre,
Vulcan Road, Leicester, LE5 3EF
www.foxeyepublishing.com

Copyright © 2024 Fox Eye Publishing
All rights reserved. No portion of this book may be
reproduced in any form without permission from the
publisher, except as permitted by U.K. copyright law.

Author: Katherine Eason
Art director: Paul Phillips
Cover designer: Emma Bailey
Editor: Jenny Rush

All illustrations by Eszter Szepvolgyi

978-1-80445-344-5

Printed in China